THE INTELLIGENCE OF CLOUDS

The Intelligence of Clouds

Poems by

Stanley Moss

Harcourt Brace Jovanovich, Publishers
San Diego   New York   London

HBJ

Copyright © 1989, 1988, 1987, 1986, 1984, 1983, 1982, 1980 by
Stanley Moss

Library of Congress Cataloging-in-Publication Data

Moss, Stanley.
    The intelligence of clouds.

    I. Title.
PS3563.0885158   1989   811'.54   88-34708
ISBN: 0-15-144850-7
ISBN: 0-15-644800-9 (pbk.)

Printed in the United States of America

A B C D E

Cover design S. M. and Wongi Sul

ACKNOWLEDGMENTS

The American Poetry Review: "Letter to the Butterflies," "For James Wright," "Clouds," "The Seagull," "Lenin, Gorky and I."

The Graham House Review: "Centaur Song," "Homing," "Song of Alphabets," "Rainbows and Circumcision," "Krill."

Nation: "The Debt," "New York Song," "Song of Imperfection," "In Front of a Poster of Garibaldi," "Allegory of Evil in Italy."

New Republic: "Hannibal Crossing the Alps."

The New Yorker Magazine: "For Margaret," "The Bathers."

Poetry: "A Gambler's Story," "April, Beijing," "To Ariel Bloch, My Arabist Friend," "Lullaby," "Song of Imaginary Arabs," "Exchange of Gifts," "Work Song," "Following the Saints," "The Lace Makers," "The Decadent Poets of Kyoto," "Elegy for Myself."

The Times Literary Supplement: "Following the Saints," "Clouds," "I Have Come to Jerusalem," "The Seagull," "Lenin, Gorky and I."

Craft International: "The Poor of Venice," "Jerusalem, Easter 1988."

Poetry Nation (United Kingdom): "For James Wright," "In Front of a Poster of Garibaldi."

Virginia Quarterly: "The Public Gardens of Munich, 1986," "In Defense of a Friend."

Tikkun: "I Have Come to Jerusalem."

Exile: "Song for Stanley Kunitz."

Exquisite Corpse: "China Sonnet," "Jerusalem, Easter 1988."

Pequod: "Travels."

CONTENTS

ONE

Song of Alphabets   3
Hannibal Crossing the Alps   5
Letter to the Butterflies   6
The Bathers   8
Song of Imperfection   10
The Lace Makers   11
The Lesson of the Birds   13
For Margaret   14
Travels   16
Clouds   18
In Front of a Poster of Garibaldi   19
Rainbows and Circumcision   22
Centaur Song   24
Homing   25
The Geographer   26

TWO

The Seagull   31
For James Wright   33
Song for Stanley Kunitz   35
In Defense of a Friend   37
Lowell   38
The Debt   39
New York Song   42
Lenin, Gorky and I   44
The Poor of Venice   46
Allegory of Evil in Italy   47
Allegory of Smell   48

A Gambler's Story   49
Panda Song   50
Lullaby   51
The Public Gardens of Munich, 1986   52

THREE

Song of Introduction   57
Following the Saints   58
Song of Imaginary Arabs   59
I Have Come to Jerusalem   60
To Ariel Bloch, My Arabist Friend   61
Exchange of Gifts   62
Work Song   63
The Battle   65
You and I   66
The Altar   67
Jerusalem, Easter 1988   68
Elegy for Myself   71
Krill   72
The Decadent Poets of Kyoto   73
On Trying to Remember Two Chinese Poems   74
China Sonnet   76
April, Beijing   77
Walking   79

To Jane and Tobia

ONE

SONG OF ALPHABETS

When I see Arabic headlines
like the wings of snakebirds,
Persian or Chinese notices
for the arrivals and departures of buses—
information beautiful as flights of starlings,
I cannot tell vowel from consonant,
the signs of the vulnerability of the flesh
from signs for laws and government.

The Hebrew writing on the wall
is all consonants, the vowel
the ache and joy of life
is known by heart. There are words
written in my blood I cannot read.
I can believe a cloud gave us the laws,
parted the Red Sea, gave us the flood,
the rainbow. A cloud teaches kindness,
be prepared for the worst wind, be light of spirit.
Perhaps I have seen His cloud,
an ordinary mongrel cloud
that assumes nothing, demonstrates nothing,
that comforts as a dog sleeping in the room,
a presence offering not salvation
but a little peace.

My hand has touched the ancient Mayan God
whose face is words: a limestone beasthead
of flora, serpent and numbers,
the sockets of a skull I thought were vowels.
Hurrah for English, hidden miracles,
the A and E of waking and sleeping,
the O of mouth.

Thank you, Sir, alone with your name,
for the erect L in love and open-legged V,
beautiful the Tree of Words in the forest
beside the Tree of Souls, lucky the bird
that held Alpha or Omega in his beak.

HANNIBAL CROSSING THE ALPS

He urged his starving elephants upward into the snows,
the barges still smelling of Mediterranean brine,
packed with huddled troops, men of Carthage
in ice-covered armor, some wearing desert sandals
wrapped in leaves, elephants up to their necks in snow,
trumpeting, their trunks grabbing at crumbling clouds of snow.
The colossal gray boulders swayed, moved upward,
some tumbled back into the echoing ravines.
An avalanche, forests of ice fell on Africa.
In the morning soldiers gathered remnants of red and blue silk,
dry sardines and beans, gold goblets still sandy
from desert victories, live turtles meant for soup,
a tangle of chained goats and sheep meant for sacrifice.

O you runners, walkers, horsemen, riders of bicycles,
men of sense and small gesture, commuters like me,
remember Hannibal came down from the Alps
into the warm belly of Italy, and conquered.
It was twenty years later in another place,
after errors of administration and alliance,
that he poisoned himself. What is remembered?
—His colossal head asleep on the sand of Tunis,
a few dates, confusion between victories and defeats,
his elephants.

LETTER TO THE BUTTERFLIES

1

Dear Monarchs, fellow Americans,
friends have seen you and that's proof,
I've heard the news:
since summer you traveled 5000 miles
from our potato fields to the Yucatán.
Some butterflies can bear what the lizard would never endure.
Few of us have the power to flutter away from the design:
I've seen butterflies weather a storm
in the shell of a snail, and come out of nowhere
twenty stories up in Manhattan.
I've seen them struggling on the ground
—I and others may die anonymously,
when all exceptionalism is over,
but not like snowflakes falling.
This week in Long Island
before the first snowfall, there is nothing left
but flies, bees, aphids, the usual.

2

In Mexico
I saw the Monarchs of North America gather,
a valley of butterflies surrounded
by living mountains of butterflies,
—the last day for many.
I saw a river of butterflies flooding
through the valley, on a bright day black clouds
of butterflies thundering overhead,
yet every one remained a fragile thing.
A winged colossus wearing billowing silk
over a sensual woman's body

waded across the valley,
wagons and armies rested at her feet.
A village lit fires,
and the valley was a single black butterfly.

3

Butterflies,
what are you to me
that I should worry about your silks and powders,
your damnation or apotheosis,
insecticides and long-tongued lizards.
Some women I loved are no longer human.
I have a quarrel with myself for leaving my purpose,
for the likes of you, beauties I could name.

Sooner or later
I hope you alight on my gray stone
above my name and date, questioning
above my bewilderment.
Is he dreaming of a butterfly,
or is a butterfly dreaming of him?
What is this nothingness
they have done to me?

THE BATHERS

1

In the great bronze tub of summer,
with the lions' heads cast on each side,
couples come and bathe together: each touches only
his or her lover, as he or she falls back
into the warm eucalyptus-scented waters.
It is a hot summer evening and the last
sunlight clings to the lighter and darker blues
of grapes and to the white and rose plate
on the bare marble table. Now the lovers
plunge, surface, drift—an intruding elder
would not know if there were six or two,
or be aware of the entering and withdrawing.
There is a sudden stillness of water,
the bathers whisper in the classical manner,
intimate distant things. They are forgetful
that the darkness called night is always present,
sunlight is the guest. It is the moment
of departure. They dress, by mistake exchange
some of their clothing, and linger
in the glaring night traffic of the old city.

2

I hosed down the tub after five hundred years
of lovemaking, and my few summers.
I did not know the touch of naked bodies
would give to bronze a fragile gold patina,
or that women in love jump in their lovers' tubs.
God of tubs, take pity on solitary bathers

who scrub their flesh with rough stone
and have nothing to show for bathing
but cleanliness and disillusion.
Some believe the Gods come as swans,
showers of gold, themselves, or not at all.
I think they come as bathers: lovers,
whales fountaining, hippopotami
squatting in the mud.

SONG OF IMPERFECTION

Whom can I tell, who cares?
I see the shell of a snail protected by a flaw
in its design: white is time, blue-green is rot,
something emerging in the rough dust, the unused
part of a shape that is furious and calm.
In aging grasses, knotted with their being,
the snail draws near the east bank of the pond,
not because that is where the morning sun is,
but out of coastal preference, raising
a tawny knotted counterwhirl
like a lion cub against its mother's haunch,
anus of a star. But let the conch stand
in the warm mud with its horn become an eye,
suffering the passion of any snail:
a miraculous life, a death, an empty tomb.
I'd follow such a horned eye, its spores, webs,
wet ferns, and corals, lip after lip, beyond
the dry wall of my life, moon-deep in the mud,
as on that afternoon Aristotle dissecting
squid proclaimed the eternity of the world.
There is not a thing on earth without a star
that beats upon it and tells it to grow.

THE LACE MAKERS

Their last pages are transparent:
they choose to see a world behind the words,
not the words, tatting not stitching, an open page
of knots, never a closed fabric stitched by needles.
They see from the apples and pears on their plates
out to the orchard, from their tatting
to a bird with a piece of straw in his beak.
From combings transferred onto a running thread,
they make a row of rings resembling a reef,
a chain of knots, hammocks, fishnets,
things found in the hands of sailors.
Without looms, with their fingers,
they make bridal objects, knotted hairnets
seen in certain Roman bronze female portraits,
the twisted threads and knotted fringes of dusty
Egyptian wrappings, something for the cuff,
the lapel, the drawing room, nothing to wear in the cold.
They care about scrolls and variations,
a handkerchief, a design on a pillow,
a completed leaf, four ovals with connecting chains
becoming four peacocks, part of a second leaf,
as if they were promised the world would not
be destroyed, with or without paradise.

Noting the French for tatting is *frivolité*,
they make false chains, things obsolete, improper,
in search of new forms. They carry a thread
to a distant point, eight measured peacocks
of equal size with an additional thread
and the ends cut off. It has the heartless advantage
of being decorative in itself.
They sit and work in the aging light
like Achilles, hiding from his pursuers

in a dress, tatting among the women,
discovered by Odysseus offering gifts:
the women picked hammered gold leaves and bracelets,
deserted by his Gods, Achilles chose a sword.
In any fabric there are constant beginnings
and endings with cut threads
to be finished off and cut out of sight.
The lacemakers read their yellow lace,
washing and ironing it is a fine art
—beautiful a straw basket filled with laundry
and language. But shall we call gossip prophecy?
Who will turn the hearts of the fathers to the children
and the hearts of the children to their fathers?
They are unworthy of undoing the laces of their own shoes.

THE LESSON OF THE BIRDS

The Birds of Aristophanes taught me
before there was sky or earth or air,
before there was mystery or the unknown,
darkness simply entered from darkness and departed
into darkness: it moved back and forth as the sea does,
but all shells, grottos and shorelines that were to be
were darkness.

Time weathered such things,
had a secret heavy underwing;
an urge toward a warm continuum,
its odor of nests made a kind of light.
Before there was pine, oak, or mud, seasons revolved,
a whirlwind abducted darkness, gave birth,
gave light to an egg. Out of the egg of darkness
sprang love the entrancing, the brilliant.
Love hatched us commingling, raised us
as the firstlings of love. There was never
a race of Gods at all until love
had stirred the universe into being.

FOR MARGARET

My mother near her death
is white as a downy feather.
I used to think her death was as distant
as a tropical bird,
a giant macaw, whatever that is
—a thing I have as little to do with
as the distant poor.
I find a single feather of her suffering,
I blow it gently as she blew
into my neck and ear.

A single downy feather is on the scales,
opposed by things of weight, not spirit.
I remember the smell of burning feathers.
I wish we could sit upon the grass
and talk about grandchildren
and great-grandchildren.
A worm directs us into the ground.
We look alike.

I sing a lullaby to her about her children
who are safe and their children.
I place a Venetian lace tablecloth
on the grass, of the whitest linen.
The wind comes with its song
about things given that are taken away
and given again in another form.

Why are the poor cawing, hooting,
screaming in the woods?
I wish death were a whippoorwill,
the first bird I could name.
Why is everything so heavy?
I did not think
she was still helping me to carry
the weight of my life.
Now the world's poor are before me.
How can I lift them one by one in my arms?

TRAVELS

1

Once I took a yellow cab up Jew mountain
to a Golgotha of telephone poles,
I saw a horizon of lovers
suffering a hundred different deaths,
I saw time as a mother in the lap of her mother,
kiss, give suck as women do in the beginning
—their hands made the wetness they touched.
I had them both and a Magdalene.

Three Marys, oh what confusion!
I went into time and women like entering a synagogue
—they kept telling me what to do.
Above me, higher than the darkness,
stained glass windows told another story:
the speaking of the flesh, the *parlando,* the *hablar.*
I waded across a river, a book in my belt,
a child on my shoulder.

What have women taught me, my beautiful teachers,
after all that lovemaking, that bathing?
How to read, dress and keep clean. Sweet one,
it is time to take on the inconveniences,
time to make and repair,
ways of kindness and deception,
ways to go to funerals and weddings
—*toujours la tendresse.*

2

It's a spring day near the Atlantic—
the sky as blue as her eyes,
time undresses before me,
moves like a girl
lifting her blouse over her head.

Now the quarrel really begins:
I tell her I have no complaints so far,
I'm not really speaking for myself
—that I don't want her to go.
I've seen the suffering she caused her lovers,
their utter humiliation.
Yes, old men and young boys,
old women and young girls.

Naked, she takes a mouth full of wine
—smiling her wicked rose-petal smile,
her eyes an endless intelligent blue,
she leans over me, and from above
pushes the wine into my mouth
—then puts her hand to my lips
as if to tell me
I was saying the wrong thing.

CLOUDS

Working-class clouds are living together
above the potato fields, tall white beauties
humping above the trees, burying their faces
in each other, clouds with darker thighs,
rolling across the Atlantic. West,
a foolish cumulus hides near the ocean
afraid of hurricanos.
Zeus came to the bed
of naked Io as a cloud,
passed over her and into her as a cloud,
all cloud but part of his face
and a heavy paw, half cloud, half cat
that held her down.
I take clouds to bed that hold me
like snow and rain, gentle ladies,
wet and ready, smelling of lilac hedges.
I swear to follow them like geese,
through factory smoke,
beyond the shipping lanes and jet routes.
They pretend nothing—opening, drifting, naked.
I pretend to be a mountain
because I think clouds like that.
A cloudy night
proclaims a condition of joy.
Perhaps I remember a certain cloud,
perhaps I bear a certain allegiance
to a certain cloud.

IN FRONT OF A POSTER OF GARIBALDI

1

When my Italian son
admired a poster of Garibaldi
in the piazzetta of Venice,
a national father in a red shirt,
gold chain, Moroccan fez and fancy beard,
I wished the boy knew the Lincoln
who read after a day's work,
the honesty, the commoner.
My knees hurt from my life and playing soccer
—not that I see Lincoln splashing with his kids
in the Potomac. Lord knows where his dead son led him.

2

My son tells me *Fortuna* could have put
Lincoln and Garibaldi in Venice—
Garibaldi in red silk, Lincoln
in a stovepipe hat black as a gondola.
My son mimics Garibaldi:
"Lincoln you may be the only man in the piazza
to log down the Mississippi
and walk back the 1500 miles to Illinois
but you are still a man who calls all pasta macaroni.
How do you know where you are going?
Your shoes are straights, no lasts,
no right or left, no fashion, white socks.
How can the President of the United States
make such a *brutta figura?*"

I can't speak for Lincoln,
any more than I can sing for Caruso
—toward the end when Caruso sang,
his mouth filled with blood.
Not every poet bites into his own jugular:
some hunger, some observe the intelligence of clouds.
I was surprised to see a heart come out
of the torn throat of a snake. I know a poet
whose father blew his brains out
before his son was born, who still leads his son
into the unknown, the unknowable.

My son tells me I must not forget
Garibaldi fought for liberty in six countries
including Uruguay, he refused the command
of a corps that Lincoln offered, asked
to be head of the Union armies and for
an immediate declaration against slavery,
he was the "King's flag," defeated
the papal armies in 1866,
which gave the Jews equality in Italy.

I've always had a preference
for politics you could sing
on the stage of the Scala.
I give my son Lincoln and Garibaldi
as guardian angels.
May he join a party and a temple
that offer a chair to the starving and unrespectable.
We come from stock that on the day of atonement

asks forgiveness for theft, murder, lies, betrayal,
for all the sins and crimes of the congregation.
May he take his girls and bride to Venice,
may the blessings come like pigeons.
Lincoln waves from his gondola and whispers,
"I don't know what the soul is,
but whatever it is, I know it can humble itself."

RAINBOWS AND CIRCUMCISION

1.

He might have made some other sign,
but it fitted his purpose to use sunlight
behind rain to make his sign of the covenant,
a rainbow, above the flood. What was in the sky
was suddenly moral, moonlight and passing clouds
were merely beautiful.

We answer the rainbow with an infant son,
cut a touch of ignorant flesh away.
The wordless infant stands on the Book
that separates him by the width of the pages
from the bookless ground.

Rainbow and mother, tell me who I am!
We might have used another sign,
a red dot on the forehead, or a scar on the cheek,
to show the world who we are,
but our sign is intimate, for ourselves
and those who see us naked—like poetry.

2.

Once in Rome, on a winter day after a rare snowfall,
I stood on a hill above the snow-covered arches,
columns, and palm trees of the pillaged Forum.
Against a dark purple sky suddenly opened
by shafts of sunlight, I saw two rainbows.

To see all that at the same time, and two rainbows,
was a pagan and religious thing: holy,
it was like the thunderous beauty of a psalm, and like
peeking through the keyhole with the masturbating slaves,
watching Hector mounted on Andromache. O rainbows!

CENTAUR SONG

A creature half horse, half human,
my father herded his mares and women together
for song, smell, and conversation. He taught me
to love wine, music, and English poetry.
Like the Greeks he left the temple's interior
for priests, he observed outside
where he could see the pediment and caryatids.
If he saw a beauty out walking, or on a journey,
the proper centaur offered to carry her
over ice, or across a river—he'd bolt
to the edge of a wood, a place of sunlight,
the light itself stunned and entertained.
He slid her gently down his back,
held her to him with one hand and a hoof.
His hoofs cut: how could he touch with tenderness?
I feel his loneliness when I am just with horses,
or just with humans. There was a time
when he was tied to a tree,
so he could not go to either.
Now his city crushed deep in the ground
has disappeared in darkness
—which is a theme for music.
He licked the blood from a trembling foal,
he galloped back to his books.

HOMING

On a bright winter morning
flights of honking geese
seem a single being
—when my kind comes into such formation
I watch for firing squads.
I never saw a line of praying figures take flight.
On an Egyptian relief I've seen
heads of prisoners facing the same direction,
tied together by a single rope
twisted around each neck
as if they were one prisoner.

I reach for a hand nearby.
An old dream makes me cautious:
as an infant, howling and pissing across the sky,
I was abducted by an eagle,
I remember the smell of carrion on its breath,
I was fed by and kissed the great beak...
Now a ridiculous, joyous bird
rises out of my breast,
joins the flock, a spot on the horizon.
I am left on earth with my kind.
They tie us throat to throat down here
—unspoken, unspeakable.
Again the honking passes over my roof.
A great informing spirit kneels overhead,
gives the mind a little power over oblivion.

THE GEOGRAPHER

Before the geography of flowers and fruit,
he learned warmth, breast, wetness.
He came late to map-making, the arches and vaults
of the compass, a real and unimagined world
of prevailing winds, coastlines and mountains,
large bodies of water, rifts and faults,
altitudes and depth. Under the stars
he studied what he learned as a child:
that geography determined history,
that weather defined places, principal products.
He would simply walk out of doors to find
the Jews of the wind arguing with the Jews of the dust:
who shall be placed among the writings,
who among the prophets, what is legend
and what is visionary dream.

He studied the deserts, the once dry Mediterranean,
the colossal sculpture of Egypt and Assyria,
an art larger than life that outweathered its gods.
Under *climate* his notes linked the Armada,
the entry "Arid Castile had nothing,
had to conquer the world,"
to Napoleon leading his infantry and dragoons
into the Russian winter, to a flock of sheep
stained with red paint that seemed to have a leader.

He learned and relearned touch, flesh, and place,
the simple "where is," the colors of nearness,
the light and dark of naked bodies in repose.
He had a small globe of the earth, he kept
inside another blue and silver globe of stars.
He tried his hand at landscape and the nude,
he learned countries and cities as if

they were words, meaning beyond subject:
the word poetry came from the Greek "to make,"
the Chinese character for poetry is "to keep."
A fine day does not forget lightning and thunder.
Memory makes any place part illusion.

He came to a certain calm in his studies
of the healing and destroying power of water,
forest fires, followed by new unheard-of growth:
he recorded bougainvillea and oleander
crossing continents like vacationing lovers,
he sketched the universe as an animal belly
of exploding gases.
He had to make it all human as a bad joke.

He knew the birds, fish, and animals
had been there before him.
He needed to know the difference
between here and there.
He had cause to be frightened,
to turn his head to the beauty of it,
away from the loneliness and betrayal.
The weather remembers, has a long memory for itself,
oceans, and countryside, something human.

TWO

THE SEAGULL

1

When I was a child, before I knew the word
for a snowstorm, before I remember
a tree or a field,
I saw an endless gray slate afternoon coming,
I knew a bird singing in the sun
was the same as a dog barking in the dark.
A pigeon in a blizzard fluttered
against the kitchen window
—my first clear memory of terror,
I kept secret, my intimations
I kept secret.

This winter I hung a gray and white stuffed
felt seagull from the cord of my window shade,
a reminder of good times by the sea,
of Chekhov and impossible love.
I took comfort that the gull
sometimes lifted a wing in the drafty room.
Once when looking at the gull I saw
through the window a living seagull glide
toward me then disappear—what a rush of life!
I remember its hereness,
while inside the room
the senseless symbol—
little more than a bedroom slipper—
dangled on a string.

Beyond argument, my oldest emotion
hangs like a gull in the distant sky,
eyes behind mud and salt
see some dark thing below:
on a trawler off Montauk
after all these years:
we headed home cleaning our fish,
the seagulls flying among us
taking the heads, spines, and guts.
A little above the Atlantic
we raced together toward the cliffs.
I felt for a few seconds, my fear and soul
flew with their cries.

FOR JAMES WRIGHT

Hell's asleep now.
On the sign above your bed
nothing by mouth,
I read *abandon hope.*

You sleep with your fist clenched,
your tongue and throat swollen by cancer,
make the sound of a deaf child
trying to speak, the smell
from the tube in your belly
is medicinal peppermint.

You wake speechless.
On a yellow pad your last writing
has double letters—two Zs and Ys in "crazy,"
you put your hand on your heart
and throw it out to me.
A few pages earlier you wrote
"I don't feel defeated."

In your room without weather,
your wife brings you more days,
sunlight and darkness, another summer,
another winter, then spring rain.

When Verdi came to his hotel in Milan
the city put straw on the street
below his window

so the sound of the carriages
wouldn't disturb him—if I could,
I'd bring you the love of America.

I kiss your hand and head, then I walk out on you
past the fields of the sick and dying
like a tourist in Monet's garden.

SONG FOR STANLEY KUNITZ

Creature to creature,
two years before we met
I remember I passed his table
at the Cedar Tavern.
He who never knew his father
seemed to view all strangers
as his father's good ghost,
any passing horse as capable
of being Pegasus, or pissing
in the street.
I who knew my father
was wary of any tame raccoon
with claws and real teeth.

At our first meeting 26 years ago,
before the age of discovery,
I argued through the night
against the tragic sense of life;
I must have thought God wrote in spit.

I keep a petrified clam, his gift, on my desk.
How many times have I kissed the stone for luck,
listened for the voice of the clam,
smelled it for what smell may reveal,
held it to my cheek in summer.
These gray rings and layers of stone,
the shape of a whale's eye,
old as any desert, place me in time.
Measured against it, the morning, the Hudson River
outside my window are modern and brash;
the star of David, the cross, the hand of Fatima,
are man-made weather vanes.

My old clam stands for periodicity,
is my sweet reminder
of heartbeat and poetry, seasons, tides, music,
all phases of all moons, light-years, menses.
Tomorrow I shall wear it for one of my eyes,
a monocle for my talk on the relationship
between paleontology and anthropology.

Bless Celia, the cat of his middle years,
with her ribbons and hats, her wet tongue,
a single note of Scarlatti, barely heard.
Bless the bobcat that was his in boyhood,
that killed a police dog in battle
on Main Street, Worcester, lost a foot for it
and had to be shot. A child with a leaf in his head
he walked through Scabious Devilsbit,
Marshrag wort, Vernal grass
until the meadows wept. Bless his first garden,
his bird feeder still there after 65 years.
How many of his long forgotten kindnesses
altered history a little?

What a *Luftmensch* he might have been,
his feet barely touching Commercial Street,
dancing home at three in the morning
with an ocean of money!
But how could he face the moon, or the land
beside his house without a garden? Unthinkable.
I think what is written
in roses, iris and trumpet vine
is read by the Lord God.
Such a place of wild and ordered beauty,
is like a heart that takes on the sorrows
of the world... He translates into all tongues.

IN DEFENSE OF A FRIEND

They say my old friend is "a good man with a worm in him."
An old revolutionary, he denies his least good fortune.
Owning his home makes him uncomfortable,
and it's true he slept in a fruit crate with his sisters,
that he believes the working class sees a different sunset.
No one will deny his life of wild love
has left him caring, with a sweet intimacy
few others have. When I took him fishing,
he wouldn't put a worm on his hook.

LOWELL

He needed to be held, so his country
held him in jail a while, non-violent,
manic New Englander. In conversation
his hands moved across sentences, a music
of almost indiscernible Latin consonants
and Tennessee cake-walking vowels.
What was sight but a God to fool the eye?
Although he looked at you he stared away,
his eyes moved across some distant lawn
like the eyes on a peacock's tail.
Now his life of love, books and nightmares,
seems 19th century American allegory,
without the lofty language.
Could he imagine the lives of those who read
without the slightest attention to form,
the lives of readers of newspapers, books
of passing interest, or nothing at all
—their deaths a slip of the tongue?
A generation that might kill itself,
gathered in him as if he were a public place:
to pray, agitate and riot. The man and flame he was
waved back and forth in the wind,
became all tongue.
In Ireland his last morning, *Whack. Huroo.*
Take your partners. Caught without time
to tell what happened, locked in a museum,
he tried to break through the glass door.
That evening in Manhattan he fell breathless
on the floor of a taxi, the meter running.
Gluck said of early opera, *It stinks of music.*
Cal, your life stank of poetry . . . . *Buzz, buzz,* he said,
a few bring real honey to the hive.

THE DEBT

1

I owe a debt to the night,
I must pay it back, darkness for darkness
plus interest.
I must make something out of almost nothing,
I can't pay back by just not sleeping
night after night. I hear them screaming
in the streets of New York, "What? What? What?"

I can't write a check to the night,
or a promissory note: "I'll write songs."
Only the nightmare is legal tender.
I bribe owls, I appeal
to creatures of the night: "Help me
raccoons, catfish, snakes!"
I put my head in the tunnel of a raccoon,
pick up a fish spine in my mouth.
Perhaps the night will accept this?
Dying is my only asset.

These days driving along I turn up my brights.
I love and am grateful for anything that lights
the darkness: matches, fireworks, fireflies.
My friend who's been to Antarctica
tells me when the sun is high against the ice
you see the shadow of the earth.
The night after all is just a shadow . . .
The debt keeps mounting.
I try to repay something by remembering
my Dante, the old five and ten thousand lira notes

had Dante's face etched on the front.
(I bought that cheap.) Hard cash to the night
is finding out what I do not want to know
about myself, no facts acceptable,
a passage through darkness,
where the one I stop to ask "Why? What?"
is always myself, I cannot recognize.

2

If only I could coin nightmares:
a barnyard in Asia,
the last dog and cat betrayed, are no more.
A small herd of three-legged blind cows
still gives milk.
A pig with a missing snout, its face like a moon,
wades in a brook.
A horse, its mane burnt to cinders,
a rear hip socket shot off, tries to get up,
thrusting its muzzle into the dark grass.
A rooster pecks without a beak or a coxcomb.
A rabbit that eats stones, sips without a tongue,
runs without feet.
A ditch of goats, sheep and oxen
locked in some kind of embrace.
All move their faces away,
refuse the charity of man
the warrior, the domesticator.
I see a whale with eyes yards apart
swimming out of the horizon,
surfacing as if it were going to die,
with a last disassociated vision,

one eye at peace
peers down into the valleys and mountains
of the ocean, the other eye floats,
tries to talk with its lids to the multitude.
While in the great head
what is happening and what happened mingle,
for neither has to be.
I pray for some of my eyes to open
and some to close.
It is the night itself that provides
a forgiveness.

NEW YORK SONG

On the way to visit a friend
who would soon suddenly die,
I saw a pigeon on a heap of rubble
standing more like a gull,
others in wild flight
searching the wreckage
of two Times Square theaters,
razed to build a hotel.
They were looking for their roof,
their nest, their young,
in the hollows of broken concrete,
in the pink and white dust,
they fluttered around the wrecking ball
that still worked the facade,
the cornice of cement Venetian masks.

A lot of people on this earth
have never sat down at a table
with a plate before them,
a knife, a fork, and a glass.
I'll be no messenger for pigeons.
It means little that I see
the obvious resemblance
between their markings
and the yellow, red and blue dots
that speckle the trout and butterfly,
a connecting phlegm between
eggs, spawn, sperm,
beauty and vanity, Helen
and Clytemnestra born
of a single egg, mortal mother
and a swan—that the roof, a giant bird
of tarpaper fallen, takes its last breaths
on the broken stage.

There are no tragic pigeons.
I mourn my sweet friend
fallen among the young,
unable to sustain flight,
part of the terrible flock,
the endless migration
of the unjustly dead.

LENIN, GORKY AND I

1

That winter when Lenin, Gorky and I
took the ferry from Naples to Capri,
nobody looked twice
at the three men having a lemon ice
in Russian wool suits hard as boards.
Behind us, a forgetful green sea,
and the Russian snows storming the winter palace.
We descended, three men a bit odd,
insisting on carrying our own suitcases
heavy with books: Marx, Hegel, Spinoza.
We took the funicular
up the cliffs of oleander and mimosa,
yet through the fumes of our cheap cigars
we observed how many travelers had come
to Capri with a beauty. Lenin to Gorky:
"In Moscow they'd kill on the streets for the girl
who showed me my room."
Within an hour of our arrival
we were sitting in the piazza drinking fizz,
longing for the girls strolling by:
a mother, a sister, a daughter.
You could smell an ageless lilac in their hair.
Lenin warned, raising our level from low to high,
"Love should be like drinking a glass of water...
You can tell how good a Bolshevik she is by
how clean she keeps her underwear."

2

It was then I split with the Communist Party.
Gorky welcomed the arrival of an old flame
from Cracow. Lenin bought white linen trousers
but would not risk the Russian Revolution
for what he called "a little Italian marmalade."
It was I who became the ridiculous figure,
hung up in the piazza like a pot of geraniums,
not able to do without the touch, taste and smell
of women from those islands in the harbor of Naples.

THE POOR OF VENICE

The poor of Venice know the gold mosaic
of hunger, the grand architecture of lice,
that poverty is a heavier brocade
than any doge would shoulder. To the winter galas
the poor still wear the red silk gloves of frostbite,
the flowing cape of chilblain.

The winged lion has his piazza, lame dogs
and pigeons with broken wings have theirs.
Let the pigeons perform for dry corn
their Commedia dell'Arte in the palms of tourists.
The rich and poor don't share a plate of beans.

There used to be songs about squid and sardines
in love the poor could make some money from.
A boy in bed with his family asks for a violin,
his father leaps up,
"Violin, violin, I'll buy you a shovel!"
Moored in the dark canals of Venice,
gondolas for prisoners, for the sick,
gondolas for the dying, the hungry,
tied to poles by inescapable knots
looped by Titian.

Salute an old Venetian after his work,
eating his polenta without quail; he sits
on a slab in the freezing mist, looking back
at the lagoon and his marble city:
years of illusion, backache, sewerage, and clouds.

ALLEGORY OF EVIL IN ITALY

The Visconti put you on their flag: a snake
devouring a child, or are you throwing up a man
feet first? Some snakes hunt frogs, some freedom of will.
There's good in you: a man can count years on your skin.
Generously, you mother and father a stolen boy,
to the chosen you offer your cake of figs.
A goiter on my neck, you lick my ear with lies,
yet I must listen, smile and kiss your cheek
or you may swallow the child completely. In Milan
there is a triptych, the throned Virgin in glory,
placed on the marble below, a dead naked man
and a giant dead frog of human scale on its back
—there's hope. My eyes look into the top of my head
at the wreath of snakes that sometimes crowns me.

ALLEGORY OF SMELL

His smile says he has had the smell of it,
flying the bitter end of a rooster tail
above his hat. In a torn army jacket
an old soldier pounds the tavern table.
They bring him an onion, garlic and a rose.
He discards the rose. He says, "To hell and back
a man stinks of what he is." He shouts:
"I myself am a sack of piss—thanks to brandy
mine smells like an apple orchard."
He remembers the gardens of women:
summer women, when they pass they enter
a man's soul through the nostrils, the consolation
the good Lord provides old soldiers.
A smell can be as naked as a breast.
His red eyes shine with tears from the onion he eats.

A GAMBLER'S STORY

There was a risk, a dividing of waters,
there was an Irish Jew whose father arrived
in Belfast from Kovno, heard English,
got off the boat and was in Ireland three years
before he discovered he wasn't in England.
His face was something like a distant sky,
his eyes were so restless one looked like the moon,
the other a sunset. Unlucky, he lost the money
for a rainy day, their daily bread, did time, then vanished.
His daughter waited all her life for the miracle
of his return, offered comfort to those beyond reason
who hoped for riches of all sorts. Years passed,
the son played roulette in Monte Carlo,
won 100,000 pounds on red 3,
gave it to his wife and children, disappeared
in Provence, where he studied mystical
philosophy, the universe still on a roll,
the greatest of all crap shoots,
the earth winning the familiar waters, the stars
taking the heavens, and darkness was the big winner.

PANDA SONG

I hear the panda's song,
on lonely afternoons
he strips bamboo with a false thumb,
uooh, uooh,
an inefficient contraption, part of his wrist,
while his real thumb is committed,
uooh, uooh,
for evolutionary and historical reasons,
to other work, mostly running and clawing,
uooh.

Neither lover nor patriot there is a cricket,
err, err,
that left in Puerto Rico
lives out its days,
err,
that dies if moved, *err,*
off its sugarcane island,
to Santo Domingo, Curaçao or Florida.
Err . . . . . . uooh, uooh,
small matters the law does not correct,
uooh, err, err.

LULLABY

I hear a Te Deum of...who are you to think...
touch religion like a hot stove,
hide bad news and the dead....a fool will light candles,
a fool will bless the children, a fool is ceremonious.

I see my first roadside wildflowers,
the lake—every sunfish nibble is a kiss.
On a summer afternoon
the clouds and I are useless brothers;
Eros carves his bow with a kitchen knife.

I read by the light of fire blazing in their hands:
my father who I thought would die forever,
my mother who I thought would live forever.
I won't forget the child who could not speak his name,
Rossini arias, the condoms on the floor,
the studying, the sweet and sour of moral purpose,
under a frowning etching of Beethoven.
The cuckoo clock was moved from room to room.
Age ten, I flew a red flag for revolution
in my bedroom and yearned for a better world.

I've made my family into an entertainment.
Once I named their symbols: the sewing basket,
fruits and animals, as their attributes.
I could show us as we were at home,
walking across a New York street or at the ocean
each brooding alone in the sand.
There is a lullaby children sing to the old.
The truth is, now in death we hold hands.

THE PUBLIC GARDENS OF MUNICH, 1986

The park benches, of course, are ex-Nazis.
They supported the ass of the SS
without questioning; the old stamp *Juden Verboten*
has been painted out.
The only signs of World War II, photographs,
displayed at the classical Greek museum,
show its roof bombed, now handsomely repaired,
although the sculpture itself has been overcleaned
by a very rough hand.

But the flowers are the children of other flowers,
the hypocrite roses and the lying begonias,
part of gardens so sentimental, so ordered,
they have nothing to say about freedom and beauty,
nothing to say about the burning bush.
They should see the flowers on the hills of Judea,
pushing between limestone and gypsum, ordinary
beautiful flowers with useful Hebrew names,
useful to children, old people, everyone,
their colors and grace, the poetry of them,
page after page.

A man can hide under his shirt
flowers made by metal and fire, stems cut,
neck wounds, missing bone, history
of generations, new branches grafted
onto old stumps.
The saying goes in the streets of Munich:
"Wear a good overcoat." Everyone knows,
you can put a dead body under a handkerchief.
Every handkerchief's a grave,
that's why so many gentlemen wear clean handkerchiefs
in their breast pockets. For the ladies, lace gloves

serve the same purpose—blue handkerchiefs, pink gloves,
green, lavender, *und so weiter,* are symbolic,
—but you have to really know—white for Jew,
blue for Jew, green for Polack, pink for
—you'd better watch out, a little joke.

This year in the Spanish garden during Carnival
someone decapitated a donkey,
Renaissance symbol of the Old Testament,
or perhaps the meaning is, as the TV
commentary said: the donkey
stands for a fifteenth-century Jew,
or was it just *Kinderspiele,*
a game like this hee-haw.

THREE

SONG OF INTRODUCTION

Ancient of Days,
I hear the sound and silence, the *lumière*
of molds, disease and insects, I believe poetry
like kindness changes the world, a little.
It reaches the ear of lion and lamb, it enters
the nest of birds, the course of fish, it is water
in the cupped hands of Arab and Jew.
Reader, in writing this I become you, I must awake
in your darkness and mine, and sleep with your sleep
and mine. If ever in writing I become a tree
I am not likely to set myself afire,
as a stone I will not stone the innocent
or guilty, my Arabs and Jews will do
what my imagination wishes: make peace.
If you bring the flood, I will dam you up
as a river, though I do it on lined paper,
with an awkward hand. I believe something is thundering
in the mold, churning the hives of insects,
that the breath of every living creature mixes
in a kiss of life, that no breath is so foul
it is not altered by the desire of the word.

FOLLOWING THE SAINTS

From the rock of my heart a horse rose,
that I should ride to follow them,
the night they left by taxi
from the Damascus gate, and fled toward Bombay.
My heart threw me off.
If only I had robes white enough,
but my robes were full of ashes and dust.
The rouge, lipstick, and eyeshadows
you left on my flesh, I washed off before prayer.
My heart was gone, it looked back at me
from a distance, its reins bitten through.

SONG OF IMAGINARY ARABS

It is written man was created,
born not of the son, but a blood clot.
When I am put in the grave and those
who question the dead ask me was the blood
drawn from the finger of God, or the heart,
or the tongue, I will not answer.
I'll say, I've heard music so beautiful
it seemed the blood of the Lord.
I know there is profit in God's word,
in silk and wool, in prayer rugs,
blood of the lamb and spit of the worm.
What does a dealer in rugs and brass trays
know of accidents and substances, the clouds
of occurrence? I prize most a brass tray
pure as the sun without etching or design,
where I first saw the angel of mathematics,
the stateless angel of astronomy.

I HAVE COME TO JERUSALEM

I have come to Jerusalem
because I have a right to,
bringing my family who did not come with me,
who never thought I would bring them here.
I carry them as a sleeping child to bed.
Who of them would not forgive me?
I have come to Jerusalem to dream
I found my mother's mother by chance,
white-haired and beautiful, frightened behind a column,
in a large reception room filled with strangers
wearing overcoats. After forty-two years
I had to explain who I was. "I'm Stanley
your grandson." We kissed and hugged and laughed,
she said we were a modern family,
one of the first to ride on trains.
I hadn't seen before how much she looked like
her great, great granddaughter. I remembered
that in her house I thumped her piano,
I saw my first painting, a garden, by her lost son.
I remembered the smells of her bedroom:
lace-covered pillows, a face powdered Old Testament.
Then my dead mother and father came into the room.
I showed them whom I'd found and gave everybody chocolates,
we spoke of what was new
and they called me only by my secret name.

TO ARIEL BLOCH, MY ARABIST FRIEND

Almost forty years after it happened
in the winter of 1947,
I saw a snapshot of my lost brother,
a Hellenistic Jew, sitting in a lifeboat,
wordless, a few yards from the shoreline of Palestine,
behind him a rusty sinking freighter,
his two years in a displaced persons' camp,
his two years in Treblinka.
With him in the boat, half a dozen Jews,
tired to death and hopeful, my brother
sat in the middle, somehow a little apart,
in a good overcoat, his gloved hands
in his pockets, thumbs out, his tilted fedora
brim up, a clean handkerchief in his breast pocket
as our mother taught him—still the *boulevardier*,
the *flâneur*. Knee deep in the water
to meet the boat and help them in, Mr. Kraus
from Frankfurt, to give the newcomers his card,
directing them to his Viennese pastry shop,
the best in Palestine.

And that other photograph of three or four
SS men, laughing, cutting off the sidelocks
of a wordless Jew wearing his prayer shawl
in a street of Vienna, and the passersby
laughing, it wasn't routine at all;
they loved every minute of it.
All this is hearsay.
My brother washed more than one death
out of his handkerchief. For me as a child
his handkerchief was a white mouse
he set free in Europe's worst winter,
when it became inhuman to love.

Ariel, whose language am I speaking?

EXCHANGE OF GIFTS

You gave me Jerusalem marble,
gypsum from the Judean desert,
granite from the Sinai,
a collection of biblical rock.
I gave you a side of smoked salmon,
a tape of the Magic Flute
—my lox was full of history and silence,
your stones tasted of firstness
and lastness, Jewish cooking.

You took me where a small boy came up to me
and asked me to dance him on my shoulders.
So we danced around Genesis and the Songs
of Solomon. He clapped his hands to be riding
the biggest horse in Judea. I cantered lightly
around Deuteronomy, whirled around the Psalms,
Kings and Job. I leapt into the sweaty
life-loving, Book-loving air of happiness.

Breathless I kissed the child and put him down,
but another child climbed up my back.
I danced this one around Proverbs and that one
around Exodus and Ecclesiastes,
till a child came up to me
who was a fat horse himself, and I had to halt.

What could I give you after that?
—When I left, a bottle of wine, half a bottle of oil,
some tomatoes and onions, my love.

WORK SONG

As full of Christianity
as the sea of salt,
the English tongue
my mother and father spoke,
so rich in Germanic tree and God worship
and old Romantic Catholic nouns,
does not quite work for me
at family burials or other,
as we say in English,
sacramental moments.

Although I know the Pater Noster
and Stabat Mater as popular songs,
I am surprised, when close friends
speak Hebrew, that I understand nothing.
Something in me expects to understand them
without the least effort,
as a bird knows song.
There is a language of prayers unsaid
I cannot speak.
A man can count himself lucky these days to be alive,
an instrument of ten strings,
or to be gently carried off by sleep and death.

What of belief? Like the tides
there is and is not a temple of words
on which work continues.
Unsynagogued, unschooled, but lettered,
I drag a block of uncut marble—

I have seen prayers pushed
into the crevices of the West Wall,
books stacked against the boulders,
ordinary men standing beside prophets and scoundrels.
I know the great stoneworkers can show the wind in marble,
ecstasy, blood, a button left undone.

THE BATTLE

When Yahweh spoke to me, when I saw His name
spelled out in blood, the pounding in my heart
separated blood from ink and ink from blood,
and Yahweh said to me, "Know your soul's name
is blood and ink is the name of your spirit.
Your father and mother longed with all their hearts
to hear my Name and title given to every generation."
When I heard the clear difference between my spirit
and my soul, I was filled with great joy,
then I knew my soul took the hillside
under its own colors, in the mirror red as blood,
and that my spirit stood its ground in the mirror
that is black as ink, and that there raged
a ferocious war in my heart between blood and ink.
The blood was of the air and the ink of the earth
and the ink defeated the blood, and the Sabbath
overcame all the days of the week.

(after Abraham Abulafia, 13th century Hebrew poet)

YOU AND I

You are Jehovah, and I am a wanderer.
Who should have mercy on a wanderer
if not Jehovah? You create and I decay.
Who should have mercy on the decayed
if not the creator? You are the Judge
and I the guilty. Who should have mercy
on the guilty if not the Judge? You are All
and I am a particle. Who should have mercy
on a particle if not the All?
You are the Living One and I am dead.
Who should have mercy on the dead if not
the Living One? You are the Painter and Potter
and I am clay. Who should have mercy on clay
if not the Painter and Potter? You are the Fire
and I am straw. Who should have mercy on straw
if not the Fire? You are the Listener
and I am the reader. Who should have mercy
on the reader if not the Listener? You
are the Beginning and I am what follows.
Who should have mercy on what follows
if not the Beginning? You are the End and I am
what follows. Who should have mercy
on what follows if not the End?

(after an anonymous 13th century Hebrew poem)

THE ALTAR

One by one I lit the candles of nothingness,
a candle for each nostril, the eyes, and ears,
a candle for the mouth, penis, and anus.
Under the clouds of nothingness,
below the flaming particles of the universe,
I stood beside the nothing tree,
I ate my fill.

To God I swore nothing.
In the blood and fires of without
nothing was written. I heard the sermons of nothing
and I knew nothing had come, and would come again,
and nothing was betrayed.

I called prayer
the practice of attention: nothing was
the balance of things contrary.
Disobedient, I did not make
the sacrifice of the lamb or the child.

My candelabrum was ablaze.

JERUSALEM, EASTER 1988

To Chana and Yehuda

1

The first days of April in the fields
—a congregation of nameless green,
those with delicate faces have come
and the thorn and thistle,
trees in purple bloom,
some lifting broken branches.
After a rain the true believers:
cacti surrounded by yellow flowers,
green harps and solitary scholars.
By late afternoon a nation of flowers: *Taioun,*
the bitter sexual smell of Israel,
with its Arabic name, the flowering red clusters
they call *Blood of the Maccabees,*
the lilies of Saint Catherine cool to touch,
beside a tree named *The Killing Father,*
with its thin red bark of testimony.
In the sand a face of rusted iron
has two missing eyes.

2

There are not flowers enough to tell,
over heavy electronic gear
under the Arab-Israeli moon,
the words of those who see a footprint
in rock of the Prophet's horse,
or hear the parallel reasoning
of King David's harp,
or touch the empty tomb.
It is beyond a wheat field to tell

Christ performed two miracles: first he rose,
and then he convinced many that he rose.

For the roadside cornflower
that is only what it is,
it is too much to answer
why the world is so, or so, or other.
It is beyond the reach
or craft of flowers to name
the plagues visited on Egypt,
or to bloom into saying why
at the Passover table Jews discard
a drop of wine for each plague, not to drink
the full glass of their enemy's suffering.
It is not enough to be carried off by the wind,
to feed the birds, and honey the bees.

3

On this bright Easter morning
smelling of Arab bread,
what if God simply changed his mind
and called out into the city,
"Thou shalt not kill," and, like an angry father,
"I will not say it another time!"
They are praying too much in Jerusalem,
reading and praying beside street fires,
too much holy bread, leavened and unleavened,
the children kick a ball of fire.

I don't know what's happening,
it's as if I were in a battle.
I catch myself almost praying
for the first time in my life,
to a God I treat like a nettle
on my trouser cuff.

The wind and sunlight commingle
with the walls of Jerusalem,
are worked and reworked, are lifted up,
have spirit, are written,
while stones I pick up in the field
at random, have almost no spirit,
are not written.

Is happiness a red ribbon on a white horse,
or like the black Arabian stallion
I saw tethered in the courtyard of the old city?
What a relief to see someone repair
an old frying pan with a hammer,
anvil and charcoal fire, a utensil worth keeping.
God, why not keep us? Make me useful.

ELEGY FOR MYSELF

The ashes and dust are laughing, swaddled,
perfumed and powdered, laughing at the flowers,
the mirrors they brought to check his breath,
and he no longer singular.
Who will carry his dust home in merriment?
These things need a pillow, a clay pot, a wife,
a dog, a friend. Plural now he is all the mourners
of his father's house, and all the nights and mornings too.
Place him with *they love* and *they wrote,*
not *he loves* and *he writes.* It took so much pain
for those "S"'s to fly off. It took so much trouble
to need a new part of speech. Now he is
something like a good small company of actors;
the text, not scripture, begins, "I am laughing."

KRILL*

The red fisherman
stands in the waters of the Sound,
then whirls toward an outer reef.
The krill and kelp spread out,
it is the sea anemone that displays the of,
the into, the within.
He throws the net about himself
as the sea breaks over him.
The krill in the net and out of it,
follow him. He is almost awash
in silver and gold.
How much time has passed!
He believes the undulation of krill
leads to a world of less grief,
that the dorsal of your smelt,
your sardine, your whitebait, humped
against the ocean's spine, cheers it
in its purpose.
The krill break loose, plunge down
like a great city of lights. He is left
with the sea that he hears
with its *if* and *then,* *if* and *then,* *if* and *then.*

*a small crustacean, basic food of the whale

THE DECADENT POETS OF KYOTO

Their poetry is remembered for a detailed calligraphy
hard to decipher, less factual than fireflies in the night:
the picture-letters, the characters, the stuff
their words were made from were part of the meaning.
A word like "summer" included a branch of plum blossoms,
writing about "summer in a city street"
carried the weight of the blossoming branch,
while "a walk on a summer afternoon"
carried the same beautiful purple shade.

They dealt with such matters distractedly,
as though "as though" were enough, as though
the little Japanese woman with the broom
returning to her husband's grave to keep it tidy
was less loving than the handsome woman in the cafe
off the lobby of the Imperial Hotel
who kissed the inside of her lover's wrist.
In their flower arrangements, especially distinct
were the lord flower and emissary roses

—public representations now shadows.
Their generals and admirals took musicians
with them to war, certain their codes
would not be deciphered, in an age when hats
and rings were signs of authority and style.
They thought their secrets were impenetrable,
they thought they had the power to speak and write
and not be understood, they could hide the facts
behind a gold-leaf screen of weather reports.

It was Buddha who had an ear for facts:
coins dropping into the ancient cedar box,
hands clapping, the sound of temple bells and drums.
Codes were broken, ships sank, men screamed
under the giant waves, and a small hat
remained afloat longer than a battleship.

ON TRYING TO REMEMBER
TWO CHINESE POEMS

1

I've forgotten the book, the poet,
the beauty of the calligraphy,
the poems made to be seen and read out loud,
two lost songs on hanging scrolls
stolen by foreigners...

2

White as frost,
a piece of freshly woven silk
made a fan, a bright moon.
She or my lady, kept a fan nearby,
its motion a gentle summer breeze,
...he dreaded the coming of autumn
when the north wind breaks the summer heat
and the fan is dropped unwanted
into a lacquer box,
its short term of favor ended.

3

A catalog of beds:
riverbed, flower bed, family bed,
...my mother died when I was three,
dreadful to be a child in baby clothes.
...I climbed into her bed and tried to nurse,
clutching her body with all my strength;
not knowing she was dead I spoke to her,
called to her. I remember thinking,

before, when I wept and ached for her,
although she was sick she came to me,
she whispered and caressed me,
then the lamp went out
and my mother coughed by the chilly window.

4

...A night of restless birds.
Without warning
a great forest fire, a devouring flaming wind,
rolling mountains of fire
with nothing to stop them but the sea.
Woman is half the sky.

CHINA SONNET

On a red banner across the center of this poem
there is painted in gold Chinese letters:
"Strive to Build Socialist Spiritual Civilization."
On the right side hangs a red banner saying,
"Intellectuals: Cleaning Shithouses for Ten Years
in the Cultural Revolution Clears the Head."
Down the left side is pasted
a lantern-thin red and black paper-saying,
"When Spring Comes Back, the Earth Is Green."
Off the page is China: the people give little importance
to what they call "spring couplets," the paper-sayings
pasted with wheat flour and water above the lintels
and down the sills of peasant houses. They seldom notice
they enter and depart through the doors of poetry.

APRIL, BEIJING

Some of the self-containment of my old face
has been sand-blasted away. The "yellow wind"
is blowing and my mouth and face burn
from the Gobi dust that scorches the city
after its historic passage over the Great Wall.
When I was young, I hosed the Atlantic salt
off my body—the salt was young too.

In China, "ashes to ashes and dust to dust"
means something more; work, no matter how cruel,
is part prophecy, workers in the same field—
with the same wooden plow
that was Chinese 8000 years ago—
the shape of a character in calligraphy,
face ashes and dust, whose windy fortress
takes on a spiritual form: the Great Wall.
In China, I can taste the dust on my own grave
like salt. The winter coal dust shadows every wall
and window, darkens the lattice and the rose,
offers its gray society to the blue cornflower,
the saffron crocus, the red poppy.

              The moon
brushed by calligraphy, poetry and clouds,
touched, lowered toward mortality:
to silk, to chess, to science, to paper,
requires that the word and painting respond
more intimately to each other, when the heart
is loneliest and in need of a mother,
when the ocean is drifting away,
when the mountains seem further off.

The birds sing in the dark before sunrise
because sunlight is delayed by dust and the sound
of a poet grinding his own ink from stone
according to the moon's teaching.
I am happy to be here, even if I can't breathe.
The emperor of time falls from a tree,
the dust rises.

WALKING

1

His stride is part delusion.
They laugh at him, "A little water in the boot,
he thinks he walks on water."
At home to get a cup of coffee
he walks across Norway, and his talk—
he speaks intimately to crowds,
and to one as a crowd. On principle
he never eats small potatoes.
Illusion, mirage, hallucination:
he loves a night painting of two figures
with fire in hand, on the grinning man's shoulder
a baboon with chain around its neck,
a reminder that art apes nature.
When they told him reality is simply what is,
it was as though he had climbed Sinai,
then walked down to get the laws.
He dreams only of the migrations of peoples
beneath the migrations of birds,
he wakes to new nations, he yawns
riddles of the north and south wind,
whistles his own tune in the holy sepulchre.
Some afternoons he stretches out in a field
like an aqueduct, "All we do," he says,
"is carry a bucket or two of God's waters
from place to place."

Under a roof, and in the open air,
hangs an amusing tragedy, a kind of satyr play,
but not every fat man dancing by
is wrapped in grape leaves. Facing himself
in an old brass mirror like the one
the ancient Chinese thought cured insanity,
tongue-tied he speaks to his own secret face,
or standing in the sunlight
against the lives of mountains, sky, and sea,
he speaks made-up and masked, the lyrical truth,
the bare-faced lie. In this century
during the wars for the survival of peoples
civilians not knowing what to do
said, "Let's do it like in the movies."
Not speaking the language of his fathers
a hero may die because all flesh is grass
and he forgets the password.

From a lectern, or top of a hay wagon,
or leaping down,
a few steps away from everyday life,
into something like a kitchen garden
he unearths in the wordless soil
things sung or said, kinds of meaning:
what is denoted or symbolic,
or understood only by its music,
or caught on to without reason,
the endless twisting of its roots, its clarity,
—aware of the old meaning of looking
to the Last Judgment,
that nothing is merely or only.

3

At a garden party he almost said,
"Madame, it is not in the bones of a lover or a dog
to wait as long as the bleached mollusk shell
on the mountain. Time is an ice cube melting
in a bowl, the world is refracted, ridiculous.
In life, you often reach out for a stone
that isn't where you see it in the stream."
But it was summer—
no one would believe time was so cold
on a hot day, so comforting,
when the purple iris was already dry
and the tulips fallen.

ABOUT THE AUTHOR

Stanley Moss was born in New York City. He was educated at Trinity College and Yale University. He has published two previous books, *The Wrong Angel* (Macmillan) and *The Skull of Adam* (Horizon) in the United States, and each with Anvil Press, London. He makes his living as a private art dealer, largely in Spanish and Italian old masters, and is the publisher and chief editor of The Sheep Meadow Press, a non-profit press devoted to poetry.